THE MAKING OF EDEN

Published by -
Dyllansow Truran,
Croft Prince,
Mount Hawke, Truro
Cornwall TR4 8EE

Printed by -
R. Booth at the
Troutbeck Press,
Antron Hill,
Mabe, Penryn
Cornwall TR10 9HH

ISBN 1 85022 143 X (cased)
ISBN 1 85022 144 8 (paperback)

my first visit to Watering Lane - the nursery where all the plants are being grown for Eden...

3

The first thing that hits you about the Nursery is that the plants are
housed in state of the Art Glasshouses. Warm & cossetted. The people

4

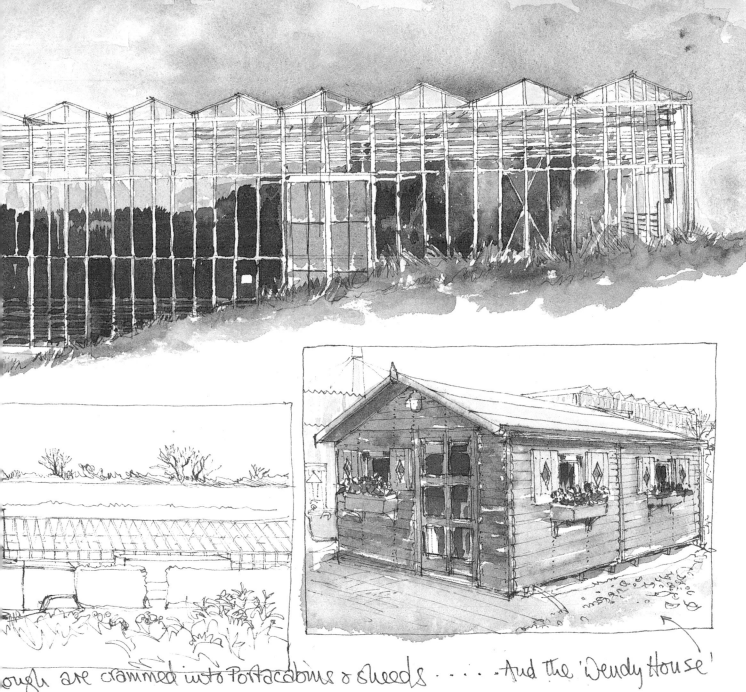

ough are crammed into Portacabins & sheds . . . . . And the 'Wendy House'

6

Orange trees with gnarled old olives behind

eden project

outside is a cornish winter
wind howling, rain beating
down.
in here all is calm
quiet & warm

7

In Glasshouse
@ 22 —
The nursery for tropical plants
Marc, whose speciality is Asiatic, rainforest
trees, says that the workers on the
'Green Team' follow all their plants through
from seedlings to eventually caring for them
in the brows. I'm beginning to see plants
in a different way

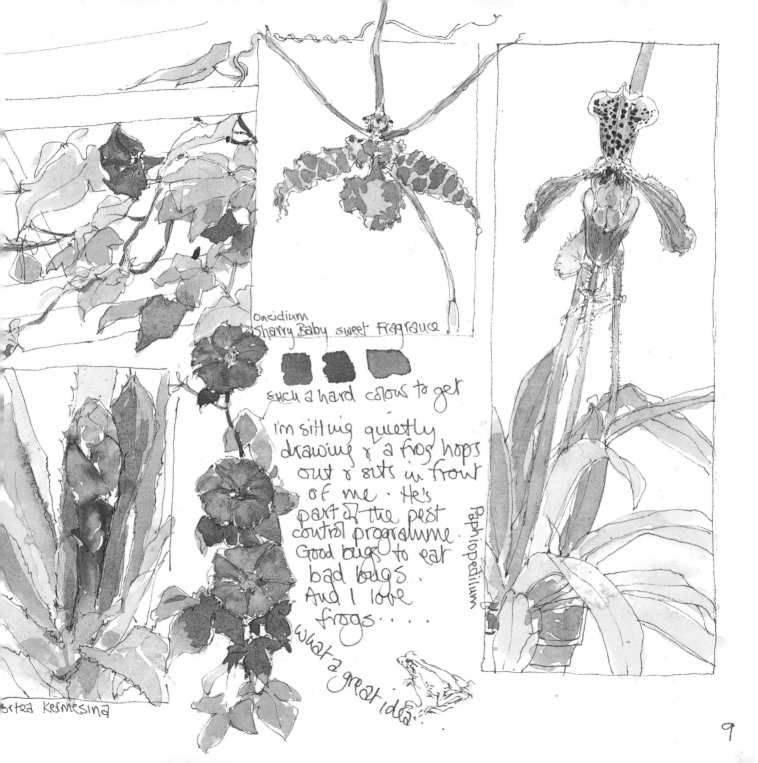

oncidium
Sharry Baby sweet fragrance

such a hard colour to get

I'm sitting quietly
drawing & a frog hops
out & sits in front
of me. He's
part of the pest
control programme.
Good bugs to eat
bad bugs.
And I love
frogs....
what a great idea.

Paphiopedilum

brtea kermesina

9

The official photographer

Watering
Nurs'
PLANT

1 LITRE IX

by spacemen riding Quad bikes – 'green' sprays as much as possible

Two things tie all the workplaces together – the plants – of course – r the coffee cups . . .

Planting, tending, watering, watching, caring... oh, & paperwork.

11

12

Plants – in glasshouses – Reflected in glasshouses · with plants –
in glasshouses ·
Reflected · in ·

13

Talking about the wiring... I think —
in amongst the orange trees.

Work table in the
shade of a
hairy-trunked
tree.

I've never seen so many plant pots there are +thousands

And thousands of them... everywhere...

15

'CORN' means cornucopia · · wt?   All these notices are on pillars across the glasshouse. I like the idea that I can walk from South Africa to California in no time at all · · · · · · ·
· · · · r on to Amazonia · ·

From the Tropics to the Med

This pink is no where near pink enough.

17

My first visit to the site —
the biggest hole in the ground
I've ever seen. It's windy & wet, with
thick, pale, creamy mud everywhere.
Down in the bottom are huge machines
that look like tiny toys. The glasshouses are
growing — giant chicken netting shapes.
I need to come back to try to understand
the scale of it all.

19

20

There's mud

or mud...

V 55 COLOUR MONITOR

22

And more mud.

here are puddles . . . r there are BIG puddles . . .

The men are slowly turning the same colour as the mud!

23

these shapes are so difficult to draw, what they must be like to build I can't imagine...

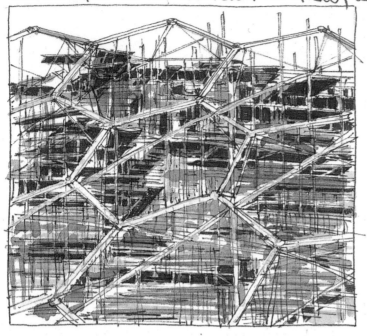
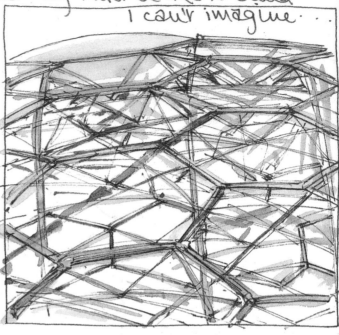

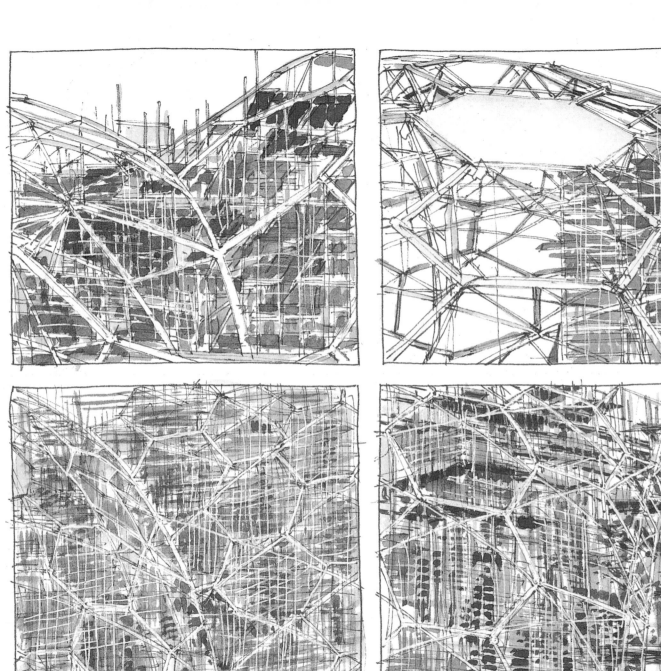

25

26

Reflections in the visitor centre - they seem to make the building disappear & expand the view. A view of mud & rubbish at the moment - but I can imagine it all . . . .

of course it's not all outside work. There's a maze of desks & filing cabinets, piles of papers & computers everywhere. I can understand the thrill of working with the plants, this, though looks tough!

i'd rather be outside...

The people may be crammed in —
but the cat gets a chair to himself.

This one looks a bit like the frog I saw in one of the glasshouses.

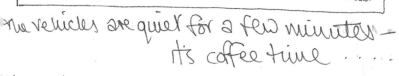

The vehicles are quiet for a few minutes — it's coffee time . . . .

The mess shed

These look like pretty ordinary trees to me – r dead at that . . .
But I guess they're not because they're all crated up r
carefully propped. It's too muddy to get to them to see
if they have any labels . . .

Oranges, lemons, limes . . . . . . r this . . . . .

Its called Buddha's Hand citron I've found our . .

Hibiscus & other exotic flowers & trays of tiny cyclamen.

It's mid-winter - what pleasure to work in glasshouses full of summer flowers & exotic fruits.

All around are the kind of plants, with exotic leaves, that you might have in a pot at home, only these are ... well ... Bigger

I had one on the windowsill - I touched it one day & all the leaves fell off - this one is HEALTHY ...

This is a weeping fig - nearly 5' high...

oh - mine was about 9" high & a little less bushy!

36

we have Arum lilies at home but they're very tiny compared with this one

I have a horrible feeling this isn't actually an Arum — I should have looked at the label

one tiny toadstool picked out by a beam of light

57

80 years old
olive trees
25' high &
weighing about 12 tons
Brought over in their
pots, from Sicily.

38

when they arrived, one of these trees had thirty oranges on it.
they didn't last long . . . r were sweeter r juicier than any
you can buy . . . (apparently . .)

Row upon row, indoors r out., soft r feathery plants,
spiky plants, tall r tiny, green r grey, blue r red.

l numbered r named,   All loved r cared for . . .

Huge leaves all shapes & sizes & every shade of green

In the Tropical House...

43

February – the weather has turned too cold for these succulent r

A little hangover from
christmas

pikey things... they're now
being cossetted in the
mediterranean House...

45

these are the smallest Narcissi
ive ever seen...

each flower head is about the
size of my little fingernail...

yellow orchids are
almost dismissed as common, but the tiny narcissi
next to them are shown off with delight by their 'minder'!

46

The site is very muddy, but parts of the nursery are far behind...

47

I was told the other day that teachers can no longer call this a 'Wendy' House - it is now officially a 'Play' House, but I don't think that will go down too well with the people who work in it ... So.. The Wendy House it remains - with cyclamens in the windowbox.